HANDS ON LAB MANUAL TO EXPLORE C# .NET

DO CODING-BUILD CONFIDENCE

GARIMA JOSHI

PRASHANT PANSE

To my Husband,Mr.Abhinav Joshi
for your endless patience, love, and belief in me.
To my lovely children Atharv and Arnika, who always make me alive and enthusiastic to learn
And to all the eager coders and my students—this book is for you.

Contents

Part 1

Foreword

What sets this book apart is its emphasis on real-world applications. I have often seen learners struggle to connect theoretical knowledge with practical implementation. This book addresses this gap head-on, encouraging readers to roll up their sleeves and engage directly with the material. The carefully crafted exercises and projects not only reinforce key concepts but also empower readers to build their own applications, transforming knowledge into tangible results.

The journey of learning programming is not merely about writing code; it's about problem-solving, creativity, and persistence. Garima Joshi instills these values throughout the chapters, inspiring readers to think critically and innovate as they explore the capabilities of C# and .NET. This book is a testament to the idea that anyone, regardless of their starting point, can become a proficient developer with dedication and the right guidance.

Preface

The importance of C# with .Net technology is very well known to Computer Science Engineers. Readers can build their concepts for the programming through this book. This book is the outcome of the problems faced by IV semester students while learning .Net. The world of programming is constantly evolving, and C# with .NET has become one of the most powerful and versatile frameworks for building modern applications. From desktop software to web applications and services, C# has proven itself as a reliable and robust language for developers at all levels. This book, , was written with one goal in mind: to provide a hands-on, practical guide for those looking to deepen their understanding of C# and .NET through real-world examples.

When I started working with C# and .NET, I realized the importance of not only understanding the theory behind the language but also applying it in practical scenarios. That's why this book focuses on practical exercises and projects that will take you from basic concepts to building fully functioning applications. Each chapter is designed to help you not only learn but also experiment and apply what you've learned, step by step.

Thank you, the reader, for choosing this book as your companion on your C# and .NET journey. I encourage you to code along, experiment, and most importantly, have fun with the learning process. I hope this book helps you take your development skills to the next level and opens new doors in your programming career.

Wish you a very happy and prosperous life and career ahead!

Acknowledgements

This book would not have been possible without the guidance, support, and encouragement of many individuals. I am deeply grateful to everyone who has helped me along this journey.

First and foremost, my heartfelt thanks to my co-author Dr. Shilpa Bhalerao, Professor and Head CSIT department, AITR, Indore and Dr. Prashant Panse, Professor, Head, IT Department, Medi-caps University, Indore whose invaluable feedback and patience shaped this work from its early stages. Your wisdom and insight have been a constant source of inspiration.

I would also like to express my gratitude to Acropolis Institute of Technology and Research, Indore for providing the resources and environment that allowed me to complete this project. Without your support, this book would not have come to life.

A special thanks to Notionpress publishers, for your meticulous attention to detail and your unwavering commitment to excellence. Your skill and dedication made this manuscript much stronger.

To my family and friends, especially my parents Mr. Ashok Joshi and Mrs. Rajlika Joshi thank you for your love, patience, and understanding throughout this process. My in-laws LN Joshi and Mrs. Manglesh Joshi for belief in me kept me going, even in moments of doubt.

Finally, to all my readers, thank you for taking the time to engage with this work. I hope you find it as enriching to read as it was to create.

With Gratitute

Garima Joshi

Prologue

In the fast-paced world of technology, the ability to adapt and learn new programming languages is more crucial than ever. C# and the .NET framework stand at the forefront of this evolution, offering developers the tools to create robust applications across various platforms. Whether you're building a simple desktop application, a complex web service, or a mobile app, C# provides the versatility and power needed to bring your ideas to life.

This book, Hands on Lab Manual to explore C#.Net is not just another programming guide; it is a practical roadmap designed for developers eager to gain hands-on experience in C# and .NET. Here, we will explore fundamental concepts through engaging, real-world projects that challenge you to apply what you've learned in a meaningful way.

Why is a hands-on approach essential? In my experience as both a developer and an educator, I've witnessed firsthand that the best way to master programming is through practice. Concepts may seem abstract when read in theory, but when you actively engage with the code—debugging, experimenting, and problem-solving—the learning process becomes not only effective but also enjoyable. This book encourages you to roll up your sleeves and dive in, fostering a deeper understanding of the material.

Course Objective:

- Gain a comprehensive understanding of the philosophy and architecture of C-Sharp programming.
  - Understand the concept of .Net Framework and C# language fundamentals.
  - Evaluate C# OOPs concept and the .NET framework namespace contents.
    - Implement the advance features of C#.
  - Demonstrate the Windows Services and creation of DLL component.

Course Outcomes:

- Understand code solutions and compile C# projects in Dotnet framework.

-

  - Demonstrate knowledge of Object oriented concepts.

-

  - Construct accessors, object, classes, methods

-

  - Implement string manipulation and exception handling.

-

Lab-1.To demonstrate the various concepts of Classes and object in C#.

Program 1.1-WAP to demonstrate class and object by considering the following :

Classname- student

Object name- s1

Data members- stud_name(string), rollno(int), mobile(int).

Input:

using System;

namespace First

{

class Student

{

string Stud_name;

int Rollno;

int mobile;

Student(string stud_name, int rollno, int mobile)

```csharp
        {
            Stud_name = stud_name;
            Rollno = rollno;
            this.mobile = mobile;
        }
        void print()
        {
            Console.WriteLine("Student details are :");
            Console.WriteLine("Student Name " +Stud_name);
            Console.WriteLine("Student rollno " +Rollno);
            Console.WriteLine("Student monile no " +mobile);
        }
        public static void Main(string[] arg)
        {
            Console.WriteLine("Name : Nehal Jain");
            Console.WriteLine("Enrollment ID : 0827CI211120");
            int rollno=110;
            int mobile=987534;
            string stud_name = Console.ReadLine();
            Student s1 = new Student(stud_name, rollno, mobile);
            s1.print();
        }
    }
}
```

Output:

```
Name : Nehal Jain
Enrollment ID : 0827CI211120
Nehal
Student details are :
Student Name Nehal
Student rollno 110
Student monile no 987534
```

Output-1.1

Program-1.2 WAP to demonstrate multiple object by considering the following :

Classname-student

Data members stud_name(string), rollno(int), mobile(int).

Object name-s1,s2

Input:

using System;

namespace First

{

class Student

{

string Stud_name = "Nehal";

static void Main(string[] args)

{Console.WriteLine("Name : Nehal Jain");

Console.WriteLine("Enrollment ID : 0827CI211120");

Student s1 = new Student();

Student s2 = new Student();

Console.WriteLine(s1.Stud_name);

Console.WriteLine(s2.Stud_name);

}

}

}

Output:

```
Name : Nehal Jain
Enrollment ID : 0827CI211120
Nehal
Nehal
```

Output-1.2

Program 1.3 WAP to demonstrate of accessing data members of one class into other class by considering the following-

Classname1-student

Classname2-stud

Data members -stud_name(string)

Object name-s1

Input:

using System;

namespace First

{

class Student

```csharp
{
public string Stud_name = "Nehal";
}
class stud:Student
{
stud()
{
Console.WriteLine("Student name is "+Stud_name);
}
static void Main(string[] args)
{Console.WriteLine("Name : Nehal Jain");
Console.WriteLine("Enrollment ID : 0827CI211120");
Stud s1 = new stud();
}
}
}
```

Output:

```
Name : Nehal Jain
Enrollment ID : 0827CI211120
Student name is Nehal
```

Output-1.3

LAB-2.To demonstrate the concept of inheritance in C#.

Program 2.1 WAP to demonstrate single level inheritance.

Input:

```
using System;

namespace First

{

class Vehicle

{

public string type = "four wheeler";

}

class car:Vehicle

{

car()

{

Console.WriteLine("vehivle type is "+type);

}

static void Main(string[ ] args)

{Console.WriteLine("Name : Nehal Jain");

Console.WriteLine("Enrollment ID : 0827CI211120");

car myObj1 = new car();

}

}

}
```

Output:

Name : Nehal Jain

Enrollment ID : 0827CI211120

vehivle type is four wheeler

Output-2.1

Program 2.2 WAP to demonstrate multi level inheritance.

Input:

using System;

namespace First

{

class Vehicle

{

public string type = "four wheeler";

}

class car:Vehicle

{

public string col = "Red";

public void print()

{

Console.WriteLine("vehicle type is "+type);

}

}

class color:car

{

color()

{

Console.WriteLine("vehicle color is "+col);

}

static void Main(string[] args)

{Console.WriteLine("Name : Nehal Jain");

Console.WriteLine("Enrollment ID : 0827CI211120");

color Obj = new color();

Obj.print(); } } }

Output:

```
Name : Nehal Jain
Enrollment ID : 0827CI211120
vehicle color is Red
vehicle type is four wheeler
```

Output-2.2

Program 2.3 WAP to demonstrate multiple inheritance.

Input:

using System;

interface Shape

{double GetArea();

}

interface Color

```csharp
{string GetColor();
}
class Rectangle : Shape, Color
{private double length;
private double breadth;
private string color;
}
public Rectangle(double length, double breadth, string color)
{this.length = length;
this.breadth = breadth;
this.color = color;
}
public double GetArea()
{return length * breadth;
}
public string GetColor()
{return color;
}
}
class Program
{
static void Main(string[] args)
{ Console.WriteLine("Name : Nehal Jain");
Console.WriteLine("Enrollment ID : 0827CI211120");
Rectangle rect = new Rectangle(5, 10, "blue");
Console.WriteLine("Area of rectangle: " + rect.GetArea());
```

Console.WriteLine("Color of rectangle: " + rect.GetColor());

}

}

Output:

```
Name : Nehal Jain
Enrollment ID : 0827CI211120
Area of rectangle: 50
Color of rectangle: blue
```

Output-2.3

Program 2.4 WAP to demonstrate of hierarchical inheritance.

Input:

using System;

namespace First

{public class Vehicle

{public string type = "four wheeler";

public string col = "Red";

}

public class car:Vehicle

{public void print()

{ Console.WriteLine("vehicle type is "+type);

}}

public class color:Vehicle

{public void show()

{Console.WriteLine("vehicle color is "+col);

}

static void Main(string[] args)

{Console.WriteLine("Name : Nehal Jain");

Console.WriteLine("Enrollment ID : 0827CI211120");

car Obj1 = new car();

color Obj2 = new color();

Obj1.print();

Obj2.show(); } } }

Output:

```
Name : Nehal Jain
Enrollment ID : 0827CI211120
vehicle type is four wheeler
vehicle color is Red
```

Output-2.4

Lab-3.To demonstrate the concept of constructor in C#.

Program 3.1 WAP to demonstrate Parameterized Constructor.

Input:

using System;

namespace First

{

public class car{

public string model_no ;

public string model_name;

car(string model_no, string model_name)

{

this.model_no=model_no;

this.model_name=model_name;

}

static void Main(string[] args)

{Console.WriteLine("Name : Nehal Jain \n Enrollment ID : 0827CI211120");

car Obj1 = new car("ABC123","Hyundai");

Console.WriteLine(Obj1.model_no+"\n"+Obj1.model_name); } } }

Output:

```
Name : Nehal Jain
 Enrollment ID : 0827CI211120
ABC123
Hyundai
```

Output-3.1

Lab-4.To demonstrate the concept of Data Abstraction using private ,public and protected keywords in C#.

Program 4.1 WAP to demonstrate Data Abstraction Using Private Keyword..

Input:

using System;

namespace nehal

```csharp
{class Student
{
private string name="XYZ";
public void print()
{
Console.WriteLine("Hello from Student class");
Console.WriteLine("Name: " +name); } }
class Program {
static void Main(string[] args)
{
Console.WriteLine("Name: Nehal Jain");
Console.WriteLine("Enrollment No: 0827CI211120");
Student student1 = new Student();
student1.print(); } } }
```

Output:

```
Name: Nehal Jain
Enrollment No:  0827CI211120
Hello from Student class
Name: XYZ
```

Output-4.1

Program 4.2 WAP to demonstrate Data Abstraction Using Public Keyword.

Input:

using System;

namespace nehal

{class Student

{

public string name = "Jaydeep";

public void print()

{

Console.WriteLine("from Student class");

}

static void Main(string[] args)

{

Console.WriteLine("Name: Nehal Jain");

Console.WriteLine("Enrollment No: 0827CI211120");

Student student1 = new Student();

Console.WriteLine("Name: " + student1.name);

student1.print(); } } }

Output:

```
Name: Nehal Jain
Enrollment No: 0827CI211120
Name: Jaydeep
from Student class
```

Output-4.2

Program 4.3 WAP to demonstrate Data Abstraction Using Protected Keyword.

using System;

namespace nehal

{

class Student{

protected string name = "jay";}

class Program : Student {

static void Main(string[] args)

{

Console.WriteLine("Name: Nehal Jain");

Console.WriteLine("Enrollment No: 0827CI211120");

Program student = new Program();

Console.WriteLine("Name: " + student.name);

}}}

Output:

```
Name: Nehal Jain
Enrollment No: 0827CI211120
Name: jay
```

Output-4.3

Lab-5.To demonstrate the concept of Run time polymorphism.

Program 5.1 WAP to demonstrate run time polymorphism using method overriding.

Input:

```csharp
using System;
class Animal {
public virtual void show(){
Console.WriteLine("Animal class");}}
class Dog : Animal
public override void show(){
Console.WriteLine("Dog class");}}
class Cat {
public static void Main()
{Console.WriteLine("Name: Nehal Jain");
Console.WriteLine("Enrollment No: 0827CI211120");
Animal obj;
obj = new Animal();
obj.show();
obj = new Dog();
obj.show();}}
```

Output:

```
Name: Nehal Jain
Enrollment No: 0827CI211120
Animal class
Dog class
```

Output-5.1

Lab-6.To demonstrate the concept of Operator Overloading in C#

Program 6.1: WAP to demonstrate Unary Operator Overloading.

Input:

```csharp
using System;
namespace UnaryOverload {
class Calculator {
public int number1 , number2;
public Calculator(int num1 , int num2)
{number1 = num1;
number2 = num2;}
public static Calculator operator -(Calculator c1)
{
c1.number1 = -c1.number1;
c1.number2 = -c1.number2;
return c1;
}
public void Print()
{
Console.WriteLine ("Number1 = " + number1);
Console.WriteLine ("Number2 = " + number2);
}
}
class EntryPoint
{static void Main(String []args)
{
Console.WriteLine ("Enrollment : 0827CI211120");
Console.WriteLine ("Name : Nehal Jain");
Calculator calc = new Calculator(15, -25);
```

Console.WriteLine ("Before Operator Overloading");

calc.Print();

calc = -calc;

Console.WriteLine ("After Operator Overloading");

calc.Print();

}

}}

Output:

```
mono /tmp/3R2IiOT2RL.exe
Enrollment : 0827CI211120
Name : Nehal Jain
Before Operator Overloading
Number1 = 15
Number2 = -25
After Operator Overloading
Number1 = -15
Number2 = 25
```

Output-6.1

Program 6.2 WAP to demonstrate Binary Operator Overloading.

Input:

using System;

namespace BinaryOverload {

class Calculator {

```csharp
public int number = 0;

public Calculator() {}

public Calculator(int n)

{

number = n;

}

public static Calculator operator + (Calculator Calc1, Calculator Calc2)

{

Calculator Calc3 = new Calculator(0);

Calc3.number = Calc2.number + Calc1.number;

return Calc3;

}

public void display()

{

Console.WriteLine("{0}", number);

}

}

class CalNum {

static void Main(string[] args)

{Console.WriteLine ("Enrollment : 0827CI211120");

Console.WriteLine ("Name : Nehal Jain");

Calculator num1 = new Calculator(200);

Calculator num2 = new Calculator(40);

Calculator num3 = new Calculator();

num3 = num1 + num2;

num1.display(); // Displays 200
```

num2.display(); // Displays 40

num3.display(); // Displays 240

}

}

}

Output:

```
mono /tmp/3R2IiOT2RL.exe
Enrollment : 0827CI211120
Name : Nehal Jain
200
40
240
```

Output-6.2

LAB-7.To demonstrate the concept of Indexer in C#

Program 7.1 WAP to demonstrate "Indexer" in C#.

Input:

using System;

class indexerr

{

private String[] val=new string[3];

public String this[int index]

{

get

```csharp
        {
            return val[index];
        }
        set
        {
            val[index]=value;
        }
    }
}
class main
{
    public static void Main(string[] args)
    { Console.WriteLine ("Enrollment : 0827CI211120");
        Console.WriteLine ("Name : Nehal Jain");
        indexerr i=new indexerr();
        i[0]="Hello";
        i[1]="this is";
        i[2]="Nehal";
        Console.WriteLine ("Values are");
        Console.WriteLine (i[0]+" "+i[1]+" "+i[2]);
    }
}
```

Output:

```
mono /tmp/LhsC7yZWWF.exe
Enrollment : 0827CI211120
Name : Nehal Jain
Values are
Hello this is Nehal
```

Output-7.1

Program 7.2 WAP to demonstrate 1D indexer with "int" datatype in C#.

Input:

```
using System;

class indexerr

{

private int[] val=new int[3];

public int this[int index]

{

get

{

return val[index];

}

set

{

val[index]=value;

}

}
```

```
}
class main
{
public static void Main(string[] args)
{ Console.WriteLine ("Enrollment : 0827CI211120");

Console.WriteLine ("Name : Nehal Jain");

indexerr i=new indexerr();

i[0]=10;

i[1]=20;

i[2]=30;

Console.WriteLine ("Values are");

Console.WriteLine (i[0]+" "+i[1]+" "+i[2]);

}

}
```

Output:

```
mono /tmp/LhsC7yZWWF.exe
Enrollment : 0827CI211120
Name : Nehal Jain
Values are
10 20 30
```

Output-7.2

Program 7.3 WAP to demonstrate 2D indexer with "int" datatype in C#.

Input:

```csharp
using System;

class indexerr

{

private int[,] val=new int[2,2];

public int this[int row,int col]

{

get

{

return val[row,col];

}

set

{

val[row,col]=value;

}

}

}

class main

{

public static void Main(string[] args)

{ Console.WriteLine ("Enrollment : 0827CI211120");

Console.WriteLine ("Name : Nehal Jain");

indexerr i=new indexerr();

i[0,0]=10;

i[0,1]=20;

i[1,0]=30;

i[1,1]=40;
```

Console.WriteLine ("Values are");

Console.WriteLine (i[0,0]+" "+i[0,1]);

Console.WriteLine (i[1,0]+" "+i[1,1]);

```
        }

    }
```

Output:

```
mono /tmp/LhsC7yZWWF.exe
Enrollment : 0827CI211120
Name : Nehal Jain
Values are
10 20
30 40
```

Output-7.3

Lab-8. To demonstrate the concept of exception Handling in C#

Program 8.1 WAP to demonstrate Exception Handling using try catch block.

Input:

```
using System;

class program

{

public static void Main(string[] args)

{

Console.WriteLine ("Enrollment : 0827CI211120");

Console.WriteLine ("Name : Nehal Jain");
```

```
int []arr={0,2,45,65,21};

try

{

Console.WriteLine("Element at index 1 is "+arr[0]);

Console.WriteLine("Element at index 2 is "+arr[2]);

Console.WriteLine("Element at index 7 is "+arr[7]);

}

catch(IndexOutOfRangeException e)

{

Console.WriteLine("Invalid Index "+e);

}

}

}
```

Output:

```
mono /tmp/3R2IiOT2RL.exe
Enrollment : 0827CI211120
Name : Nehal Jain
Element at index 1 is 0
Element at index 2 is 45
Invalid Index System.IndexOutOfRangeException: Index was outside the
    bounds of the array.
  at program.Main (System.String[] args) [0x00062] in
      <973aabf95b6344d9bd2d4a48fbdd34cc>:0
```

Output-8.1

Program 8.2 WAP to demonstrate Exception Handling using try finally block.

Input:

```csharp
using System;

class program
{
public static void Main(string[] args)
{
Console.WriteLine ("Enrollment : 0827CI211120");

Console.WriteLine ("Name : Nehal Jain");

int []arr={0,2,45,65,21};

try
{
Console.WriteLine("Element at index 1 is "+arr[0]);

Console.WriteLine("Element at index 2 is "+arr[2]);

Console.WriteLine("Element at index 7 is "+arr[7]);
}

catch(IndexOutOfRangeException e)
{
Console.WriteLine("Invalid Index "+e);
}

finally
{
Console.WriteLine("Element at index 3 is "+arr[3]);
}
}
}
```

Output:

```
mono /tmp/3R2IiOT2RL.exe
Enrollment : 0827CI211120
Name : Nehal Jain
Element at index 1 is 0
Element at index 2 is 45
Invalid Index System.IndexOutOfRangeException: Index was outside the
    bounds of the array.
  at program.Main (System.String[] args) [0x00062] in
      <71be75f952a6417c8f7b8ebb0e3cfe57>:0
Element at index 3 is 65
```

Output-8.2

Program 8.3 WAP to demonstrate Exception Handling using throw.

Input:

using System;

class program:Exception

{

public program()

{

Console.WriteLine("Invalid Index ");

}

public static void Main(string[] args)

{

Console.WriteLine ("Enrollment : 0827CI211120");

Console.WriteLine ("Name : Nehal Jain");

int []arr={0,2,45,65,21};

int j=1;

while (j>0)

```
                    {

    Console.WriteLine("Enter Index");

    int i= Convert.ToInt32(Console.ReadLine());

    if(i>4)

    throw new program();

    Console.WriteLine("Element at index "+i+" is "+arr[i]);

                    }

                    }

                    }
```

Output:

```
mono /tmp/3R2IiOT2RL.exe
Enrollment : 0827CI211120
Name : Nehal Jain
Enter Index
3
Element at index 3 is 65
Enter Index
7
Invalid Index
Unhandled Exception:
program: Exception of type 'program' was thrown.
  at program.Main (System.String[] args) [0x00051] in
     <68dda12828ee4a729354ad18288b8de5>:0
[ERROR] FATAL UNHANDLED EXCEPTION: program: Exception of type 'program'
    was thrown.
  at program.Main (System.String[] args) [0x00051] in
     <68dda12828ee4a729354ad18288b8de5>:0
```

Output-8.3

Lab-9.To demonstrate the concept of Delegate in C#

Program 9.1 WAP to demonstrate Delegate.

Input:

```csharp
using System;

public class Myclass
{
public delegate void callback(int i);
public void longrunning(callback c)
{
for(int i=1;i<=5;i++)
{
c(i);
}
}
}
class program
{
public static void Main(string[] args)
{
Console.WriteLine ("Enrollment : 0827CI211120");
Console.WriteLine ("Name : Nehal Jain");
Myclass c=new Myclass();
c.longrunning(callback);
static void callback(int i)
{
Console.WriteLine (i);
}}}
```

```
mono /tmp/3R2IiOT2RL.exe
Enrollment : 0827CI211120
Name : Nehal Jain
1

2

3

4

5
```

Output-9.1

Lab-10.To demonstrate the Code access security in class library using DLL component.

Program 10.1 WAP to demonstrate creating class lib in C# & converting it into DLL also add reference of it in another console application thereby providing code access security.

Input:

// make a class1 in class Library

namespace CodeAccessSecurity

{

public class Class1

{

int num1, num2, result;

public int pnum1

{

set { num1 = value; }

}

```csharp
        public int pnum2
        {
            set { num2 = value; }
        }
        public int presult
        {
            get { return result; }
        }
        public void add()
        {
            result = num1 + num2;
        }
    }
}
// make a another class2
using System;
using System.Collections.Generic;
using System.Linq;
using System.Text;
using System.Threading.Tasks;
namespace CodeAccessSecurity
{
    public class Class2 // change access specifier internal to public
    {
        public int square(int x)
        {
```

```csharp
        return x * x;

    }

}

}
```

// build the program and by this it convert to ddl

// define main function in console and add project reference

```csharp
using CodeAccessSecurity;

using System;

namespace Console

{

public class program

{

public static void Main(String []args)

{

Console.WriteLine(" Name : Nehal Jain");

Console.WriteLine(" Enrollment : 0827CI211120");

Class1 o1 = new Class1();

Class2 o2 = new Class2();

o1.pnum1 = Convert.ToInt32(Console.ReadLine());

o1.pnum2 = Convert.ToInt32(Console.ReadLine());

o1.add();

Console.WriteLine("Sum is :" + o1.presult);

Console.WriteLine("Enter any number: ");

int n= Convert.ToInt32(Console.ReadLine());

Console.WriteLine("Square is : "+ o2.square(n));
```

Console.Read();

}

}

}

Output:

```
Name : Nehal Jain
Enrollment : 0827CI211120
23
34
Sum is :57
Enter any number:  .
41
Square is : 1681
```

Output-10.1

Lab-11.To demonstrate the concept of reflection in C#

Program 11.1 : WAP to demonstrate Metadata Information of about type t.

Input :

using System;

using System.Reflection;

namespace reflection

{

class refelction

{

public static void Main(string[] args)

{

Console.WriteLine ("Name: Nehal Jain");

Console.WriteLine ("Enrollment: 0827CI211120");

Type t =typeof(string);

Console.WriteLine ("Name :{0}",t.Name);

Console.WriteLine ("Full Name :{0}",t.FullName);

Console.WriteLine ("Namespace :{0}",t.Namespace);

Console.WriteLine ("Base Type :{0}",t.BaseType);

}

}

}

Output:

```
mono /tmp/qM7dAuEW96.exe
Name: Nehal Jain
Enrollment: 0827CI211120
Name :String
Full Name :System.String
Namespace :System
Base Type :System.Object
```

Output-11.1

Program 11.2 WAP to demonstrate Reflection to print metadata information of classes , methods of classes and its parameters by considering the following: Classname : book

Data members : bookname ,bookID ,year of Publication.

Input:

using System;

using System.Reflection;

```csharp
namespace reflection
{
    class book
    {
        string bookName;
        int bookID;
        int yearofPub;
        public book()
        {
            bookName = "XYZ";
            bookID = 0;
            yearofPub = 0;
        }
        public book( string Name,int ID,int year)
        {
            bookName = Name;
            bookID = ID;
            yearofPub = year;
        }
        public void display()
        {
            Console.WriteLine ("Book Name :{0}",bookName);
            Console.WriteLine ("Book ID :{0}",bookID);
            Console.WriteLine ("Year of Publication :{0}",yearofPub);
        }
    }
```

```csharp
class main
{
    public static void Main(string[] args)
    {
        Console.WriteLine ("Name: Nehal Jain");
        Console.WriteLine ("Enrollment: 0827CI211120");
        Assembly executing = Assembly.GetExecutingAssembly();
        Type[] types =executing.GetTypes();
        foreach(var item in types)
        {
            Console.WriteLine ("Class :{0}",item.Name);
            MethodInfo[] methods =item.GetMethods();
            foreach(var method in methods)
            {
                Console.WriteLine ("--> Method :{0}",method.Name);
                ParameterInfo[] parameters =method.GetParameters();
                foreach(var arg in parameters)
                {
                    Console.WriteLine ("--> Parameters :{0} Type :{1}",arg.Name,arg.ParameterType);
}}}}}
```

Output:

```
mono /tmp/qM7dAuEW96.exe
Name: Nehal Jain
Enrollment: 0827CI211120
Class :book
--> Method :display
--> Method :Equals
--> Parameters :obj Type :System.Object
--> Method :GetHashCode
--> Method :GetType
--> Method :ToString
Class :main
--> Method :Main
--> Parameters :args Type :System.String[]
--> Method :Equals
--> Parameters :obj Type :System.Object
--> Method :GetHashCode
--> Method :GetType
--> Method :ToString
```

Output-11.2

Lab-12.To demonstrate the concept of String Builder class and their methods in C#

Program 12.1 WAP to demonstrate String Builder functions: Append() , remove() , clear() , replace() , insert().

Input:

using System;

using System.Text;

class stringbuild

{

// Main Method

public static void Main()

{

Console.WriteLine("Name : Nehal Jain \n Enrollment : 0827CI211120");

// "10" is capacity

StringBuilder s = new StringBuilder("HELLO ", 10);

s.Append("Nehal ");

// after printing "Nehal"

// a new line append

s.AppendLine("Jain");

s.Append("Hello World");

s.Insert(6, "Everybody ");

s.Replace("Nehal", "Sambhav");

s.Remove(5, 3);

s.Clear();

Console.WriteLine(s);

}

}

Output:

1. **Append()**

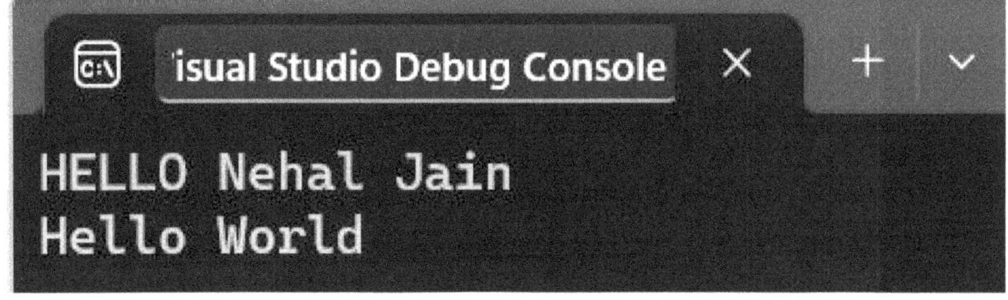

Output-12.1-Append

2.Insert()

Output-12.1-Insert

3. **Replace()**

Output-12.1-Replace

4. **Remove()**

Output-12.1-Remove

5. **Clear()**

Output-12.1-Clear

Program 12.2 WAP to demonstrate String and String Builder for displaying the time difference between both.

Input:

```
using System;

using System.Text;

using System.Diagnostics;

namespace strings

{

class stringbulid

{

public static void Main(string[] args)

{

Console.WriteLine("Name : Nehal Jain \n Enrollment : 0827CI211120");

string s = "";

Stopwatch sw = new Stopwatch();

sw.Start();

for (int i = 1; i < 100000; i++)

{ s = s + i ; }

sw.Stop();
```

```csharp
StringBuilder sb = new StringBuilder();

Stopwatch sw1 = new Stopwatch();

sw1.Start();

for (int i = 1; i < 100000; i++)

{ sb.Append(i);

}

sw1.Stop();

Console.WriteLine("Time taken for string " + sw.ElapsedMilliseconds);

Console.WriteLine("Time taken for another string " + sw1.ElapsedMilliseconds);

Console.ReadLine();

}

}

}
```

Output:

```
Name : Nehal Jain
 Enrollment : 0827CI211120
Time taken for string  31012
Time taken for another string  1
```

Lab-13.To demonstrate the concept of sending mail using SMTP in C#

Program 13.1 WAP to demonstrate sending mail with Smtp in C# by using System.Net.Mail Package and display the following output " sending email******" .

Input:

```csharp
using System;

using System.Net;

using System.Net.Mail;

namespace console

{ public class program

{ public static void Main(string[] args)

{

Console.WriteLine("Name: Nehal Jain\n Enrollment: 0827CI211120");

Console.WriteLine("hello");

SendEmail(fromAddress: GetUserName(), GetPassword());

Console.ReadLine();

}

public static void SendEmail(string fromAddress, string password)

{

using SmtpClient email = new SmtpClient

{

DeliveryMethod = SmtpDeliveryMethod.Network,

UseDefaultCredentials = false,

EnableSsl = true,

Host = "smtp.gmail.com",

Port = 465,

Credentials = new NetworkCredential(userName: fromAddress, password) };

string subject = "youtube video";
```

```csharp
string body = $"This is the main email sent @{DateTime.UtcNow:F}";

try
{ Console.WriteLine("sending email****");

email.Send(fromAddress, recipients: Toaddress(), subject, body);

Console.WriteLine(" email sent****");

}

catch (SmtpException e)

{ Console.WriteLine(e); }

}

public static string GetUserName()

{ return ""; }

public static string GetPassword()

{

return "";

}

public static string Toaddress()

{ return "";

}

}

}
```

Output:

```
Select Microsoft Visual Studio Debug Console
Name: Nehal Jain
 Enrollment: 0827CI211120
hello
sending email****
Unhandled exception. System.ArgumentException: The parameter 'from' cannot be an empty string. (Parameter 'from')
   at System.Net.Mail.MailMessage..ctor(String from, String to)
   at System.Net.Mail.SmtpClient.Send(String from, String recipients, String subject, String body)
   at console.program.SendEmail(String fromAddress, String password) in C:\Users\student\source\repos\ConsoleApp2\Consol
eApp2\Program.cs:line 35
   at console.program.Main(String[] args) in C:\Users\student\source\repos\ConsoleApp2\ConsoleApp2\Program.cs:line 14

C:\Users\student\source\repos\ConsoleApp2\ConsoleApp2\bin\Debug\net6.0\ConsoleApp2.exe (process 6116) exited with code 0
.
To automatically close the console when debugging stops, enable Tools->Options->Debugging->Automatically close the conso
le when debugging stops.
Press any key to close this window . . .
```

Output-13.1

Lab-14.To demonstrate the concept of Windows Services in C#

Program 14.1 WAP to demonstrate creation of Windows Services using C# in Visual studio.

Input:

Step 1: Open Visual Studio, click File > New, and select a project. Next, select a new project from the Dialog box, select "Window Service," and click the OK button.

Step 2: Go to Visual C# ->" Windows Desktop" ->" Windows Service," give an appropriate name and then click OK.

Step 3: Right-click on the blank area and select "Add Installer."

Step 4: Right-click on the blank area and select "View Code"

Step 5: It has a Constructor, which contains the InitializeComponent method.

Select the InitializeComponent method and press the F12 key to go to definition.

Step 6: Now add the below line:

```csharp
private void InitializeComponent()
{
    this.serviceProcessInstaller1 = new System.ServiceProcess.ServiceProcessInstaller();
    this.serviceInstaller1 = new System.ServiceProcess.ServiceInstaller();
    //
    // serviceProcessInstaller1
    //
    this.serviceProcessInstaller1.Account = System.ServiceProcess.ServiceAccount.LocalSystem;
    this.serviceProcessInstaller1.Password = null;
    this.serviceProcessInstaller1.Username = null;
    //
    // serviceInstaller1
    //
    this.serviceInstaller1.Description = "My First Service demo";
    this.serviceInstaller1.DisplayName = ".Demo";
    this.serviceInstaller1.ServiceName = "Service1";
    //
```

step-6

Step 7: In this step, we will implement a timer and code to call the service at a given time. Then, we will create a text file and write the current time in the text file using the service.

```csharp
using System.Timers;
namespace NehalJain
{
    public partial class Service1 : ServiceBase
    {
        Timer timer = new Timer(); // name space(using System.Timers;)
        public Service1()
        {
            InitializeComponent();
        }
        protected override void OnStart(string[] args)
        {
            WriteToFile("Service is started at " + DateTime.Now);
            timer.Elapsed += new ElapsedEventHandler(OnElapsedTime);
            timer.Interval = 5000; //number in milisecinds
            timer.Enabled = true;
        }
        protected override void OnStop()
        {
            WriteToFile("Service is stopped at " + DateTime.Now);
        }
        private void OnElapsedTime(object source, ElapsedEventArgs e)
        {
            WriteToFile("Service is recall at " + DateTime.Now);
        }
        public void WriteToFile(string Message)
        {
            string path = AppDomain.CurrentDomain.BaseDirectory + "\\Logs";
            if (!Directory.Exists(path))
            {
                Directory.CreateDirectory(path);
            }
            string filepath = AppDomain.CurrentDomain.BaseDirectory + "\\Logs\\ServiceLog_" + DateTime.Now.Date.ToShortDateString().Replace('/', '_') + ".txt";
            if (!File.Exists(filepath))
            {   | // Create a file to write to.
                using (StreamWriter sw = File.CreateText(filepath))
                {
                    sw.WriteLine(Message);
                }
            }
            else
            {
                using (StreamWriter sw = File.AppendText(filepath))
                {
                    sw.WriteLine(Message);
                }
```

Step-7

Step 8 : Rebuild your application.

```
Output

Show output from: Build

Rebuild started...
1>------ Rebuild All started: Project: NehalJain, Configuration: Debug Any CPU ------
1>  NehalJain -> C:\Users\nehal\source\repos\NehalJain\NehalJain\bin\Debug\NehalJain.exe
========== Rebuild All: 1 succeeded, 0 failed, 0 skipped ==========
========== Rebuild started at 10:17 PM and took 00.905 seconds ==========
```

step-8

Step 9 : Search "Command Prompt" and run as administrator.

Step 10 : Fire the below command in the command prompt and press ENTER.

cd C:\Windows\Microsoft.NET\Framework\v4.0.30319

Step 11 : Now Go to your project source folder > bin > Debug and copy the full path of your Windows Service exe file.

```
Microsoft Windows [Version 10.0.22621.1702]
(c) Microsoft Corporation. All rights reserved.

C:\Windows\System32>cd C:\Windows\Microsoft.NET\Framework\v4.0.30319

C:\Windows\Microsoft.NET\Framework\v4.0.30319>InstallUtil.exe C:\Users\nehal\source\repos\NehalJain\NehalJain\bin\Debug\NehalJain.exe
Microsoft (R) .NET Framework Installation utility Version 4.8.9032.0
Copyright (C) Microsoft Corporation.  All rights reserved.


Running a transacted installation.

Beginning the Install phase of the installation.
See the contents of the log file for the C:\Users\nehal\source\repos\NehalJain\NehalJain\bin\Debug\NehalJain.exe assembly's progress.
The file is located at C:\Users\nehal\source\repos\NehalJain\NehalJain\bin\Debug\NehalJain.InstallLog.
Installing assembly 'C:\Users\nehal\source\repos\NehalJain\NehalJain\bin\Debug\NehalJain.exe'.
Affected parameters are:
   logtoconsole =
   logfile = C:\Users\nehal\source\repos\NehalJain\NehalJain\bin\Debug\NehalJain.InstallLog
   assemblypath = C:\Users\nehal\source\repos\NehalJain\NehalJain\bin\Debug\NehalJain.exe
Installing service Service1...
Service Service1 has been successfully installed.
Creating EventLog source Service1 in log Application...

The Install phase completed successfully, and the Commit phase is beginning.
See the contents of the log file for the C:\Users\nehal\source\repos\NehalJain\NehalJain\bin\Debug\NehalJain.exe assembly's progress.
The file is located at C:\Users\nehal\source\repos\NehalJain\NehalJain\bin\Debug\NehalJain.InstallLog.
Committing assembly 'C:\Users\nehal\source\repos\NehalJain\NehalJain\bin\Debug\NehalJain.exe'.
Affected parameters are:
   logtoconsole =
   logfile = C:\Users\nehal\source\repos\NehalJain\NehalJain\bin\Debug\NehalJain.InstallLog
   assemblypath = C:\Users\nehal\source\repos\NehalJain\NehalJain\bin\Debug\NehalJain.exe

The Commit phase completed successfully.

The transacted install has completed.

C:\Windows\Microsoft.NET\Framework\v4.0.30319>
```

step-11

Output:

Open services by following the below steps:

1. Press the Window key + R.

2. Type services.msc.

3. Find your Service.

	Name	Description	Status	Startup Type	Log On As
Services (Local)					
NehaUain.Demo	Microsoft Software Shadow ...	Manages so...		Manual	Local System
	Microsoft Storage Spaces S...	Host service ...		Manual	Network Se...
Start the service	Microsoft Store Install Service	Provides infr...	Running	Manual	Local System
	Microsoft Update Health Ser...	Maintains U...		Disabled	Local System
Description:	Microsoft Windows SMS Ro...	Routes mess...		Manual (Trigg...	Local Service
My First Service demo	Natural Authentication	Signal aggre...		Manual (Trigg...	Local System
	NehaUain.Demo	My First Ser...		Manual	Local System

Final Output

Lab-15.To demonstrate the Concepts of reading and writing of XML file in C#.

Program 15. 1 WAP to reading a XML file - yourname.xml using C#.

Input:

```csharp
using System;
using System.Collections.Generic;
using System.Linq;
using System.Text;
using System.Threading.Tasks;
using System.Xml;

namespace reading_xml
{
    0 references
    class program
    {
        0 references
        public static void Main (String[] arg)
        {
            XmlDocument xmlDoc = new XmlDocument ();
            xmlDoc.Load("C:\\Users\\nehal\\OneDrive\\Pictures\\Screenshots\\Nehal.xml");
            xmlDoc.Save(Console.Out);

        }
    }
}
```

Input-15.1

Output:

```
<?xml version="1.0" encoding="Codepage - 437"?>
<breakfast_menu>
  <food>
    <name> Name: Nehal Jain </name>
    <name> Enrollment : 0827CI211120 </name>
    <name> Belgian Waffles</name>
    <price>$5.95</price>
    <description>
Two of our famous belgian waffles with plenty of real maple
</description>
  </food>
</breakfast_menu>
C:\Users\nehal\source\repos\menu\menu\bin\Debug\net6.0\menu.exe (
To automatically close the console when debugging stops, enable T
le when debugging stops.
Press any key to close this window . . .
```

Output-15.1

Program 15.2 WAP to reading a XML file elements name , price , description from Nehal.xml using C#.

Input:

```csharp
using System;
using System.Collections.Generic;
using System.Linq;
using System.Text;
using System.Threading.Tasks;
using System.Xml;

namespace reading_xml
{
    class program
    {
        public static void Main (String[] arg)
        {
            XmlTextReader xtr = new XmlTextReader("C:\\Users\\nehal\\OneDrive\\Pictures\\Screenshots\\Nehal.xml");
            while(xtr.Read())
            {
                if (xtr.NodeType == XmlNodeType.Element && xtr.Name == "name")
                {
                    string s1 = xtr.ReadElementString();
                    Console.WriteLine("Name = "+ s1);
                }

                if (xtr.NodeType == XmlNodeType.Element && xtr.Name == "price")
                {
                    string s2 = xtr.ReadElementString();
                    Console.WriteLine("Price = " + s2);
                }
                if (xtr.NodeType == XmlNodeType.Element && xtr.Name == "description")
                {
                    string s3 = xtr.ReadElementString();
                    Console.WriteLine("Description = " + s3);
                }
            }
        }
    }
}
```

Input-15.2

Output :

```
Name =  Name: Nehal Jain
Name =  Enrollment : 0827CI211120
Name =  Belgian Waffles
Price = $5.95
Description =
Two of our famous belgian waffles with plenty of real maple
```

Output-15.2

Program 15.3 WAP to demonstrate creating an XML file in C# to print an element employee ID , Name and Department.

Input:

```csharp
using System.Linq;
using System.Text;
using System.Threading.Tasks;
using System.Xml;
namespace writingfile
{
    class program
    {
        public static void Main(string[] args)
        {
            string filename = "C:\\Users\\student\\Employee.xml";
            XmlTextWriter xmlWriter = new XmlTextWriter(filename,System.Text.Encoding.UTF8);
            xmlWriter.Formatting = Formatting.Indented;
            xmlWriter.WriteStartDocument();
            xmlWriter.WriteComment("creating an XML file uisng c# ");
            xmlWriter.WriteStartElement("Employees");

            for (int i = 1; i<= 2; i++)

            {
                xmlWriter.WriteStartElement("Employee");
                Console.WriteLine("Enter the ID of Employee"+i);
                xmlWriter.WriteElementString("IO", Console.ReadLine());


                Console.WriteLine("Enter the name for employee" + i);
                xmlWriter.WriteElementString("Name", Console.ReadLine());
                Console.WriteLine("Enter the depy for employee" + i);
                xmlWriter.WriteElementString("Dept", Console.ReadLine());
                xmlWriter.WriteEndElement();
            }

            xmlWriter.WriteEndElement();
            xmlWriter.WriteEndDocument();
            xmlWriter.Flush();
            xmlWriter.Close();
```

Input-15.3

Output :

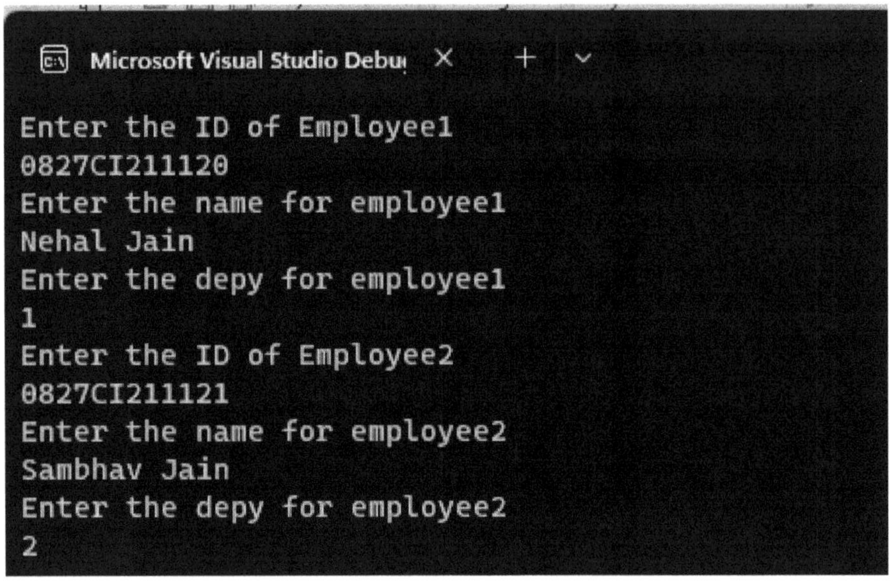

```
Microsoft Visual Studio Debu
Enter the ID of Employee1
0827CI211120
Enter the name for employee1
Nehal Jain
Enter the depy for employee1
1
Enter the ID of Employee2
0827CI211121
Enter the name for employee2
Sambhav Jain
Enter the depy for employee2
2
```

Output-15.3

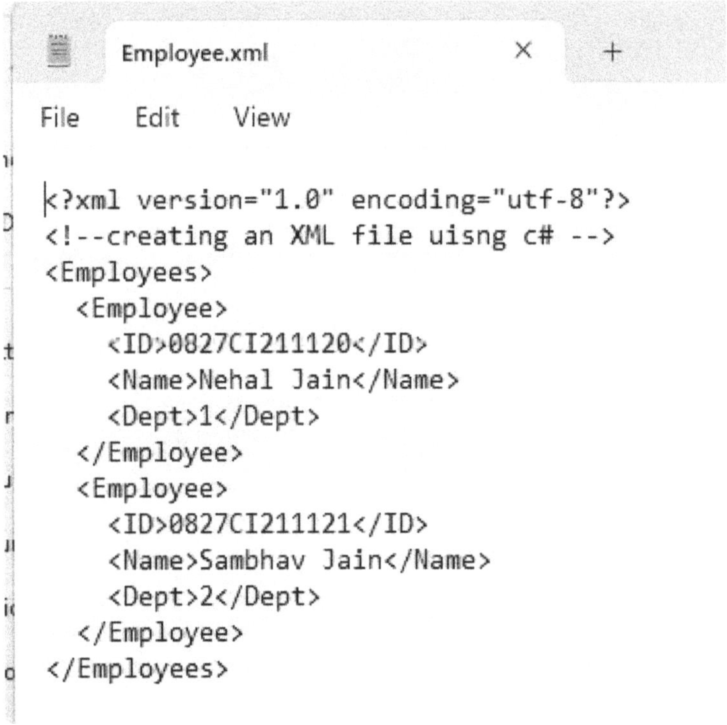

```
Employee.xml
File    Edit    View

<?xml version="1.0" encoding="utf-8"?>
<!--creating an XML file uisng c# -->
<Employees>
  <Employee>
    <ID>0827CI211120</ID>
    <Name>Nehal Jain</Name>
    <Dept>1</Dept>
  </Employee>
  <Employee>
    <ID>0827CI211121</ID>
    <Name>Sambhav Jain</Name>
    <Dept>2</Dept>
  </Employee>
</Employees>
```

Output-15.3-XML code

www.ingramcontent.com/pod-product-compliance
Lightning Source LLC
Chambersburg PA
CBHW040909130726
48005CB00019BA/3044